AF487917

the root & star Joke Book

Why didn't the teddy bear
eat lunch?

Because it was
stuffed!

What is worse than finding
a worm in your apple?

Finding HALF a worm
in your apple!

I reached for the fog
to taste it, but...

...mist.

How do fish always know
how much they weigh?

Because they have
their own scales!

How do you make
an octopus laugh?

with ten-tickles!

What's the easiest way
to catch a fish?

Have someone throw
it at you!

What did the magician
say to the fisherman?

Pick a cod, any cod!

Why did the shark
spit out the clownfish?

Because it tasted
funny!

Do you know
a fish joke?

No.

Well...let minnow
when you do!

What's an elephant's
favorite vegetable?

Squash!

What do you get
when you plant kisses?

Tulips! 

Why did the banana
go to the doctor?

It wasn't peeling well!

Why couldn't the gardener
plant any flowers?

He hadn't botany!

What is orange and sounds
like a parrot? 

A carrot! 

Chickens rise when the
rooster crows, but when do
ducks get up?

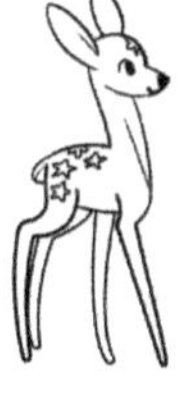

At the quack of dawn!

What would happen if we
threw books into the
ocean?

There would be a title wave!

What does it mean
if you find a horseshoe?

There is a horse
walking around
in their socks!

A cowboy arrived at the
horse farm on a Sunday. He
worked for three days and
left on Friday.
How is that possible?

His horse was named Friday!

Why did the person walk
outside with their purse open
to the sky?

Because they
expected
some change in the
weather!

How do you know
when the moon
is going broke?

It's down to its last quarter!

How does the man
in the moon
cut his hair?

Eclipse it!

What holds the moon up?

Moonbeams! 

Why wasn't the moon
hungry?

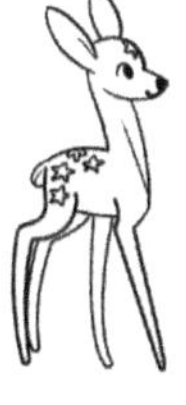

Because it was full!

What do you call a dinosaur
who doesn't give up?

A try, try, triceratops!

What do dogs love to read about?

Bark-aeology!

Why is it difficult for leopards
to play hide and seek?

Because they are always spotted!

Why did the fairy move out
of the toadstool?

Because there wasn't mushroom!

How do you get a baby alien
to sleep?

You rocket!

What type of tree
fits in your hand?

A palm tree!

How do you identify
a dogwood tree?

By its bark!

What do you get
when you cross
a sheep and a honeybee?

Baaa-humbug!

What did one happy frog
say to the other?

Time's sure fun
when you're having flies!

Why did the child throw butter
out the window?

To see the butter fly!

(don't try this at home!)

What part of a turkey is
musical?

The drumstick!

Mountains aren't just funny...

...they are hill areas!

What do you call a Frenchman
wearing sandals?

Philippe Philoppe!

Why do oranges wear sunscreen?

Because they peel!

Do you know why orange
juice is so smart?

Because it concentrates!

What kind of crows always
stick together?

Vel-crows!

Why was the crow perched
on a telephone wire?

He wanted to make
a long-distance caw!

What do crows drink
to stay awake?

Caw-fee!

Time flies like an arrow...

... and fruit flies like a banana!

How do you cut a wave
in half?

With a sea-saw!

How do geologists like to relax?

In rocking chairs!

Where do fish keep their
money?

In river banks!

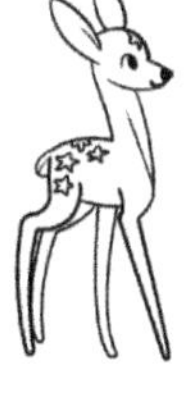

Why did the farmer
win an award?

Because he was out standing
in his field!

What did the right eye say
to the left?

Don't look now,
but something
in between us smells!

 Knock knock.

 Who's there?

 Raccoon eyes.

 Raccoon eyes who?

Don't you raccoon eyes me?! 

How do you get a piano to laugh?

You tickle the ivories!

What is an acorn?

In a nutshell,
it's an oak tree!

Is it true you can cut off a
branch just by looking at it? 

It's true. I saw it
with my own eyes!

What is a tree's
least favorite month?

Sep-TIMBERRRR!

Why was the cat
afraid of the tree?

Because of its bark!

What did the beaver say
to the tree?

It's been nice gnawing you!

When do you GO at red
and STOP at green?

When you're eating a watermelon!

What goes up
when the rain
comes down?

Umbrellas!

What bow can't be tied? 

A rainbow!

What runs but never walks?

A river!

How do you fix
a broken strawberry?

With a strawberry patch!

How did the mouse feel
after its bath?

Squeaky clean!

What goes
tick tock bow wow?

A watch dog!

What's an owl's favorite song?

Owl You Need Is Love!

With what vegetable do you
compost the outside and
cook the inside, then eat the
outside and compost the
inside?

Corn!

What is the longest word
you know?

SMILES!

There is a MILE between each "S"!

Why did the farmer wear
one boot to town?

Because she heard there was
a 50% chance of snow!

What did the 0 say to the 8?

Nice belt!

Where does the General
keep his armies?

Up his sleevies!

What did the plate
say to the fork?

Dinner is on me!

Which building has
the most stories?

The library!

How does the scientist
freshen her breath?

With experi-mints!

How do you make a tissue dance?

You put a little boogie in it!

What was T. Rex's
favorite number?

Eight! (gulp!)

Why does the seagull
fly over the sea?

Because if it flew over the bay,
it would be a bagel!

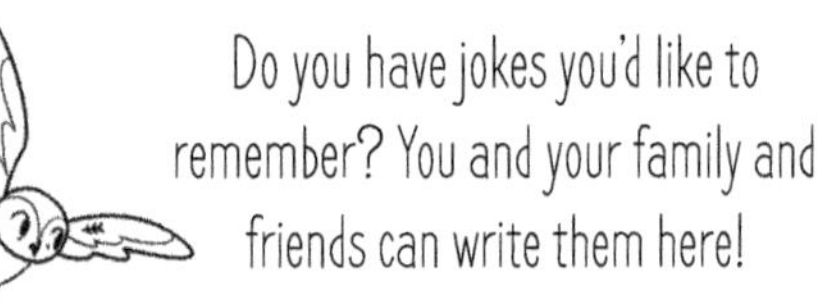

Do you have jokes you'd like to
remember? You and your family and
friends can write them here!

My Jokes

Thank you for reading!
Remember to be kind
to one another!

love,
Root & Star

Root & Star, winner of a Parents' Choice
Gold Award, originated as a magazine in
2016. We strive to nurture the connection
between grown-ups and children through
literature and art. We continue to publish
a variety of work in many forms.